IF NOT NOW, WHEN?

Richard E. Tomlinson

Copyright © 2023 Richard E. Tomlinson

All rights reserved.

No part of this book may be reproduced, stored in a retrieval system, or transmitted by any means, electronic, mechanical, photocopying, recording, or otherwise, without written permission from the author.

ISBN (Paperback): 979-8-9894070-6-4
ISBN (eBook): 979-8-9894070-5-7

I dedicate this book to all those in search of a deeper understanding of their lives, and pray this is the start of that journey.

Also, I wish to give special thanks to Granddaughters Alex, and Emma whose enthusiasm and input were extraordinary. As well, this wish extends to Kara, whose untiring ministry work with SPO improves untold lives on college campuses.

I love you all.

TABLE OF CONTENTS

Chapter 1: CONGRATULATIONS! 1

Chapter 2: THE JOURNEY BEGINS..5

Chapter 3: A PERSONAL WAKEUP CALL 7

Chapter 4: THE EXCITEMENT GROWS 9

Chapter 5: FEELING THE MESSAGE..11

Chapter 6: SOCIAL JUSTICE 15

Chapter 7: LOVE 19

Chapter 8: PEACE 23

Chapter 9: CHARACTER BUILDING 27

Chapter 10: CONFLICT RESOLUTION 33

Chapter 11: WISDOM 37

Chapter 12: JUDGEMENT...43

Chapter 13: FORGIVENESS...47

Chapter 14: COMPASSION 53

Chapter 15: FAITH 59

Chapter 16: CHOOSING A MENTOR.....................................65

Chapter 17: "LIFE MENTOR'S WISDOM AND ADVICE" 71

Chapter 18: MIRACLES...77

Appendix 1: CONSCIENCE OR CONSEQUENCES 79

Appendix 2: JUST HOW POWERFUL IS THE WORD? 85

Appendix 3: THE UNIMAGINABLE
REALLY HAPPENED 87

Appendix 4: LONELINESS IS AN EPIDEMIC
STATES THE US SURGEON GENERAL.
IS HE RIGHT? 89

Appendix 5: BONO, AND U2'S LAMENT.
THE FINAL CONNECTION..93

Appendix 6: HOMELESS..95

Appendix 7: KELLY: WHEN IS A HANDICAP A GIFT?......99

CHAPTER ONE

The Bible God's Awesome Story

CONGRATULATIONS!

You are about to take a fascinating journey into the greatest self-help book ever written in history. (Actually, it is a compilation of seventy-two books and letters, combined into one: The Holy Bible).

You say you have never read the Bible? Or, perhaps you have read it, and essentially it was interesting, or possibly boring, but not really earth-shattering. You may have glanced through various pages, not necessarily grasping the meaning or the intent of the author.

Well, either way, you are in for a life-changing treat.

First, let's talk about YOU. After all what good is a self-help book if it doesn't address your concerns and problems? It must center on your interests, needs, challenges, problems, family, and friends. Therefore, these subjects beg the following questions.

Are you interested in:

- Social Justice
- Love
- Peace
- Character building
- Interpersonal relationships
- Conflict Resolution
- Redemption
- Joy
- Wisdom and words to live by
- History
- Forgiveness
- Compassion
- Searching for life's answers
- What is faith, and how does that affect my life?
- Is there a God?
- If so, who is He?
- What happens after I die?

The Bible literally has dozens of answers to those critical subjects, most of which are very easy with which to relate, and understand. With some patience, perseverance, and an unquenchable thirst to improve and enjoy your life to the fullest, you will now be embarking on a unique and fulfilling journey.

In a nutshell, the Bible is a collection of historical and religious writings, and scriptures, revered by most cultures, particularly those with Christian and Jewish populations. Its relevance has influenced art, literature, history, culture, health, social justice, personal relationships, and family units. It is divided into two primary sections:

The Old Testament (Before Jesus Christ, and the history of the Jewish people). The New Testament, from Jesus's birth, through His life, death, and resurrection. It then continues to describe in fascinating detail, how Christianity survived, and the evolution of the development of today's church.

The Bible is the ONLY book of its kind, dating back approximately 3,700 years, and has several dozen authors most of whom were eyewitnesses to their writings. Once you become engaged in a meaningful way, it has the power to impact your life, in a long-lasting and very special, beautiful way. That is why it is referred to as a most sacred text.

Although there are many and varied editions of the Bible, the one I chose, and strongly suggest is a STUDY BIBLE. Mine happened to be a Catholic Study Bible, but there are many excellent other publications such as this one. The Catholic Bible has seventy-two books, and Letters in its contents, the Protestant version has 66. For the most part, the Bibles are mirror images of each other.

The Study Bibles include very important, and necessary background and interpretive sections that, for me, were (and remain so), irreplaceable. For example, my Bible begins with a Reading Guide for every one of the seventy-two separate contents. The RG helps you position the contents of say, the Gospel of John, in not only a historical way but how it is relevant to the story being told. As well, prior to each entry in the overall Bible, there is a brief Introductory page setting up the reading in which you are about to engage. (The term Gospel means Good News).

Finally, the Study Bible has extensive footnotes on each page that help to more clearly define words, phrases, events, and persons, and assist the reader in a timely fashion so that the meaning of that which is being read truly comes alive with much more impact.

I cannot emphasize enough how much richer and enhanced your experience will be with all the assistance given by the various study support components. I do believe that far more people would enjoy the incomparable benefits of the Bible if they followed the above advice. The Bible is far too complex to just pick it up, without these assists, and proceed on your own. The richness, power, and historical/sacred substance are just otherwise missing.

What the Bible IS NOT, is a novel, which is meant to be read cover to cover, beginning with the first page, and reading straight through. I will be discussing in subsequent chapters some of the suggested readings that I found most fascinating, which may be helpful to you. However, as you get into this fabulous book, you will more than likely find dozens of other areas that have a significant meaning for your life which I may not have highlighted.

CHAPTER TWO

God's Awesome Story

THE JOURNEY BEGINS

Ten years ago, I was in the process of moving from Phoenix, AZ to Mt. Pleasant, SC, and signed into a long-stay motel, awaiting my furniture which was going to take eight days in transit.

I awoke at 5:00 a.m. the first morning, a time I was used to since Phoenix was three hours behind the East Coast, and I had been on conference calls to Boston at 9:00 a.m. EST for the past year with a client.

As I arose in the pitch-black, small room and fumbled my way to the light switch and coffee maker, I remembered something was missing. During the previous several years I would intermittently pick up my Study Bible, open it to where I had left off, and proceed with attempting to satisfy the curiosity that had been lurking in my mind since I was in my teens as to what this book was all about.

However, there I was, in a strange motel room with nothing to read as my bible was in transit with the rest of my belongings. So, with hopeful anticipation, I went to the nightstand next to the bed, opened the drawer, and found a Gideon's Bible.

Not remembering where I had previously left off, I simply opened the book at random.

I was not ready for what happened next.

CHAPTER THREE

God's Awesome Story

A PERSONAL WAKEUP CALL

With no exaggeration or hyperbole, I was stunned.

The book opens to the first Chapter of The Gospel of John. Over many years, I read and re-read this page, dozens of times, and proceeded to read the subsequent chapters. But not this time. Something was different, very, very different.

It is a challenge to describe what happened, particularly to those who have not experienced such sensation, and it is easily thought to be an imagination run wild.

John starts by saying: "In the beginning was the Word, and the Word was God. He was in the beginning with God; all things were made through Him, and without Him, nothing was made. In Him was life, and life was the light of men. The light shines in the darkness, and the darkness has not overcome it".

Wow. What? This was written by a man who had met Jesus Christ, *IN PERSON.* Think about it. Living, walking, eating, talking, and listening to "this person", whom John found out was the God of all creation, with His Father, and the Holy Spirit. John sat down and wrote this after Christ was crucified, and rose from the dead!

However, I get ahead of myself (since the experience still excites me!). I read this over, and over, with my mind trying to comprehend the overwhelming story John was sharing. The longer I concentrated on this opening dialog, the more powerful, and expanding the words became.

I put myself in John's place, feeling I was literally there in person, living the same moments as John. Something was happening to me, and although I wasn't sure what it was, it had literally changed my life.

CHAPTER FOUR

God's Awesome Story

THE EXCITEMENT GROWS

Before we start, it is important to understand that I am no Biblical scholar, nor do I pretend to be. I am simply a man who has read the Bible dozens of times over several decades. I became at least conversant enough with some of the stories, and details so that I could understand what they were talking about when mentioned in church, or in conversation with someone else. However, my desire and intensity increased dramatically over the past ten years, once I had the experience with John's Gospel. It was not only becoming a source of fascination on cultural, and spiritual levels, but on personal levels as well. Yes, the Bible took on a whole new, powerful dimension for me. That is an excitement I want to share with you.

All my life, I have been fascinated and bewildered over not only the joys and extraordinary sorrows of mankind, but what exactly is God's role in all of our lives, and history itself. I mean, what's the purpose? Is there a purpose?

There are varying versions of a famous story, called "The Boy and The Ocean". Allow me to share it as it has a great perspective. As the story goes, the little boy is sitting on the beach, with a small shovel, and bucket. Repeatedly, he gets up, goes to the water, fills his little bucket, and returns to a small hole he has dug in the sand, whereupon he dumps the water into the hole.

Along came a stranger, and inquired as to what the boy was doing. The child said it was his intention to take all the water from the ocean and place it in the hole he had dug. It was obvious to the man that the little boy had no concept of what he was attempting to accomplish.

The moral of the story draws a parallel to our attempts to comprehend God, His purpose, life, and eternity. Impossible? Hmmm?

Maybe, however, just maybe, there really is a way we can pull back the proverbial curtain, and not only take a peek at what God had in mind before, and what He has in mind for us now…and into eternity.

Actually, He has provided that indescribable insight for us. It's called the Bible.

Ready for an incredible journey? Let's get started !!

CHAPTER FIVE

God's Awesome Story

FEELING THE MESSAGE

Suggestions as to getting the most lasting experience, while enjoying each separate reading:

- Read to FEEL the message. It took me years of reading, and re-reading the same text before that experience I mentioned at the beginning of this book, with a random opening of the Book of The Gospel of John. Please trust my experience. When I read, I place myself right into the story. I smell the desert air, feel the Israeli's pains during Exodus, am challenged by Daniel facing the lion, and am part of the audience when Jesus is speaking His everlasting words of wisdom, which originate from His Father. Wow, just Wow. What a difference that makes.

- Set aside some uninterrupted time. I realize busy schedules, family commitments, and doctor appointments are all very demanding. So, I found that getting up an hour before all the busyness starts, I was able to get at least one or two chapters of a key area I was interested in learning more about. Take "small bites". Over time, you will be amazed at how they add up to important life lessons.

- Now that I am retired, and live by myself, I have the unique privilege of getting up at 5:00 a.m. each morning and delving deeply into the Bible for about two hours. Literally, when I am in the grocery store, or cleaners, or drug store, or fast food outlet and see some of the same people on a frequent basis, they often ask, why I am always so happy. Sounds corny, but I just tell them I started the day with very special information and instruction.

- Do not be intimidated by the size and scope of the Bible. It took thousands of years to write, so take each specific book, or writing, in a very relaxed and eyes wide open way. Take your time, it's the best book you'll ever read!

- For me, not only am I sure to check the Reading Guides first, and refer to the footnotes as I go along, but I keep my handy iPhone next to me. Why? There are certain times when I want further clarification of a term, or subject, and I am able to access multiple opinions from knowledgeable people of different disciplines.

- Pace yourself, and TAKE NOTES. I find by going over my notes, I am able to refresh my memory as to why I asked a question in the first place.

- Some people prefer a Bible Study Group, and they find the camaraderie, and assistance of a group leader who is knowledgeable in the teachings to be very helpful. I suggest you do a combination of this approach, then when you are home, delve into some personal study.

- Approach a member of the clergy, either in your own church or synagogue, and ask for their assistance, and/or recommendations.
- Share your newfound excitement with family, and friends. You'll be surprised at how frequently they ask more about your interest in the Bible.
- Have a clear sense of why you are reading it, what you expect out of it, and possibly what you can do with your new insights.

The power and satisfaction you will receive for your personal life will depend upon careful reading, an open mind, a willingness to learn, an open heart, and faith that what you are reading can literally change your life and the world for the better.

Ready, set…let's get going!

CHAPTER SIX

God's Awesome Story

SOCIAL JUSTICE

Social Justice has come to the forefront of all media, particularly because of the ubiquitous social media that literally billions of people participate in and with every day.

However, this begs the question: exactly what is Social Justice, and where did it originate? Actually, it has been a major topic of prominent, powerfully wise thinkers for thousands of years. So, even though it seems to be a more nascent development, it is not.

Just what is Social Justice? It refers to the fair and equitable distribution of resources, rights, and opportunities. It ensures everyone is treated fairly, and has equal access to human needs, regardless of their background, identity, or social status.

It covers the equitable treatment of all in the areas of education, healthcare, employment, housing, and criminal justice.

Dignity, respect, equal opportunities, and love for your neighbor are foundational aspects of this concept.

Where did all this originate, and continues to predominate? The Holy Bible.

Let's look at just a few examples. In the Book of Isaiah, (Old Testament), Chapter 1, verse 17, he states: "Learn to do good, search for justice, discipline the violent, be just to the orphans, plead for the widows". And, who was this Isaiah? He was a brilliant prophet who lived about 2,700 years ago, and among other significant attributes, he accurately and precisely predicted the birth and additional details of Jesus Christ coming, 700 years before it happened!

Other prominent Social Justice advocates in both the Old and New Testaments, but certainly not limited to, were in the Gospel of Luke, Chapter 10, verses 25-37. Book of Leviticus, Chapter 25, verses 8-17, and the Prophet Micah, Chapter 6, verse 8.

St. Luke was a Greek physician, who not only chronicled Jesus's life in substantial detail but who wrote the Acts of The Apostle's Book, which further details the extraordinary lives of the men and women who traversed the known world, primarily in the Mediterranean countries, promoting the Christian ethic and doctrine, both of which were heavily involved with Social Justice. This took place 2,000 years ago. Luke's Gospel emphasizes **inclusiveness, compassion, and the power of the Holy Spirit,** to ensure it would last a lifetime.

A further example of Social Justice in the Acts of The Apostles is in Chapter 2: 42-47. "All believers were together, and had everything in common. They sold property and possessions to give to anyone who had need". Further, it states "all believers were of one heart and one mind. With great power, the apostles continued to testify to the resurrection of the Lord Jesus. And, God's grace was so powerfully at work in them that there were no needy people among them".

Finally, in the books of Leviticus, and Micah, both powerful examples of ancient Jewish philosophy, they state: "If you buy land from, or sell to a countryman, neither shall exploit the other (Leviticus 25: 8-17). And, you have been told what is right by Yahweh (God), only do this, to do what is right, to have loyalty, and walk humbly with God", Micah 6:8.

Therefore, you can see Social Justice is very prominent throughout the Bible. As you investigate further, you'll uncover many more examples, showing why the Bible has lasted thousands of years, without revision.

CHAPTER SEVEN

God's Awesome Story

LOVE

There is probably no topic more frequently discussed, misunderstood, written about, nor absolutely more confusing than… Love. We all experience it in multiple ways, possibly several times a day!

People profess to love their children, religion, certain foods, travel, mates, new cars, and of course, the list extends almost without end. Which probably, is a good thing!

However, there are two very different types of love, that are well articulated in the Holy Bible, and that are so foundational to our understanding and participation therein, that we must examine them in their own context.

Of course, romantic love is the first thought that comes to mind when discussing the subject. However, there is one much more powerful, long-lasting, and rewarding. It is the First Commandment in the Bible: "You shall love the Lord your God, with your whole heart, your whole mind, and your whole soul, and you shall worship no false Gods". (Pay particular attention to the "false Gods" statement, which emerges in a later discussion). The enormous benefits that flow from an acceptance, and commitment to this love is not only something we can experience in this lifetime, but eternally. Wow. Worth paying attention to, wouldn't you think?

The second Biblical comment on love is the Second Commandment: "Love your neighbor as yourself." Whoa!! When you really think about it, this is a really tough one. (More to come on this as well).

The term "love" itself is mentioned in the Bible approximately 280 times, so if you already consider yourself an expert on the subject, you may want to explore deeply into the various scriptures, since they all touch on the subject in one way or another. The references are to God, one another, and yourself. So, the topic has been discussed since the beginning of mankind, beginning with Adam and Eve (how'd that one work out?!).

The Biblical illustrations are truly fascinating, and so numerous that you cannot miss them. Again, they cover three primary subjects: God, your neighbor, and yourself. You'll also notice as you read through this incredible series of books/writings, that there are certain **exclusions** for love: money, possessions, ill-gotten gains, idols, power, control, your neighbor's wife and their goods, and those things that conflict with the three primary targets of love.

The Bible is replete with examples of love gone right, and love gone wrong. It provides powerful, and successful leaders such as Abraham (see his love for God in the story of his son, Issac!!), Moses (see his love for all Jewish people!!), Jesus (see His love for All Mankind and the ultimate sacrifice He gave!!). See, too, love gone wrong (check out King David and his romance with Bathsheba, another man's wife!!). Love of power, exercised inappropriately, is covered extensively in the Scriptures (see the discussion of the Babylonians, Assyrians, and of course shortly thereafter the fall of the Roman Empire. Power tends to have a very finite lifeline. Therefore, I strongly encourage all readers to enjoy a comprehensive literary exposure via a journey through Jewish history in the Old Testament.

However, to better understand the Bible's attention to the Love of God, your neighbor, and one's self, I suggest a complete reading of the following Biblical offerings.

The most powerful examples of love ever given, are clearly illustrated as follows: The Gospel of John, Chapter 3, verse 16: "For God so loved the whole world He gave His only begotten Son, so that whoever believes in Him, shall have life eternal" Wow! Can it possibly get any better than that?! Then, the most profound act of love ever recorded was when Jesus died a horrific death of crucifixion on the cross, and said He was doing that for All Mankind For The Forgiveness Of Sins. Yes, that's every human being. Now, that's a love that is so profound, it is almost impossible to comprehend. Remember, I said "almost" impossible, but as you'll see in the Book of Hebrews, Chapter 11: verse 1. Faith is the answer. Look it up, it is powerful!!

Some of the extraordinary examples of love that the reader may enjoy are the following, as well: Paul's Letter in 1 Corinthians: Paul states: If I am without love, I am nothing. Love is always patient, and kind, never jealous, not boastful nor conceited. Love finds its joy in the truth." This is just a small quote from a magnificent letter by Paul, written during the year 100.

Also, check out the Gospel of Luke, Chapter 10:25-37 where a lawyer questions Jesus and His reply refers to the ultimate love, as previously mentioned. As well as, Chapter 15:10-32 in Luke is a well-known, powerful, and incredibly introspective peek at the human mind. It is the parable of the Prodigal Son. It is a must-read, and study ALL aspects of it, including not only the father's love, but the younger son's penitential action, and the oldest son's reaction. Read carefully, there is lots to consider here, with all three participants.

Richard E. Tomlinson

This Prodigal Son parable is typical of the incredible obvious, as well as hidden meanings that are so rich in wisdom, that it must be read carefully, sometimes several times over, and as mentioned earlier, use your Reader's Guide, it is invaluable!

As you will see from 3,700 years of Biblical contributions, from dozens of extraordinary writers, most of whom were all eye-witnesses to their contributions, there is "Good" and "Bad" love. More than likely, you experience some of both frequently in your daily life.

The key is to follow the Biblical examples, and you'll find life much more peaceful, and rewarding.

Remember, these are but a few examples that I have chosen. See how many more of the 280 "love" mentions in the Bible you can find on your own.

CHAPTER EIGHT

God's Awesome Story

PEACE

"My peace I leave with you, my peace I give to you," John 14:27. These are the words spoken by Jesus Christ, himself. He then said, "Do not let your hearts be troubled," John, 14:1.

This is one form of peace, a spiritual one. People also seek a more personal inner peace, look for peace among peoples/cultures, and offer peace as a blessing. Of course, they are all interrelated.

In these troubled and tumultuous times, finding true and lasting peace in your life, or even a single day, can be an extraordinary challenge!

Social media, in particular, promulgates excessive anxiety, selfishness, and suicidal tendencies through false accusations, electronic bullying, fake news, and abnormal sexuality.

Irrespective of a person's age, when they are either physically or emotionally challenged, the peace that we all long for suddenly and dramatically disappears. Now what? Where do you go for relief? Too many people find refuge in drugs, alcohol, and dependent relationships, stripping them of their ability to determine an acceptable outcome or change of circumstances that would be to their benefit.

Well, one resource that has been used quite effectively, literally by billions of people for 3,700 years is The Holy Bible. The terms "peace, and peaceful" are not only used dozens upon dozens of times in the Bible, but they are beautifully and convincingly illustrated, as well.

As shown above, in John's Gospel, Jesus takes many opportunities when speaking with large and small crowds, to reassure them their God **does love them**, and that faith is the answer.

Yes, indeed, this was a peaceful solution to the anxiety that the Jewish people as well as the Gentiles (non-Jews) had for not only their lives but for centuries. The continual search for a Messiah, a Savior to not only protect them from marauding, hostile armies but most importantly to show them how to best live with all their fellow human beings, and ultimately be rewarded with life eternal with God Himself.

The Prophet Isaiah said it best, 700 years before Christ was born, but unquestionably relating directly to Him when referring to Him as the Prince of Peace, 9:6; "For to us a child is born, to us a son is given, and the government will be on His shoulders. And, He will be called wonderful counselor, mighty God, Everlasting Father, and **THE PRINCE OF PEACE**". So for those seeking peace, Christ is the Alpha and the Omega, the "Beginning and the End" of the search. He provides complete and total fulfillment throughout His actions, miracles, and words in the New Testament. As well, in Isaiah 26:3-4 he states: "**If you trust in God, keep your mind stayed on God. He will keep you in perfect peace because He is an everlasting rock!**"

Isaiah is also quoted as saying while addressing the leaders of a large crowd in his community: "This is the plan decreed; you will guarantee peace; the peace entrusted to you". You see, there has never been a time in the history of mankind when peace was not only necessary but an absolute priority. But, powerful peace advocacy continued well into, and after Christ's life on earth.

The Apostle Paul, who is the most prominent convert from Judaism to Christianity as he led thousands of people, often through extraordinarily challenging situations urged and pleaded for peace in his preaching, and Letters to various congregations. Two excellent examples are as follows:

Paul's Letter to the Philippians (citizens of the City of Philippi, Greece), 4:7, "and the peace of God, which is beyond our understanding, will guard your hearts, and your thought in Christ Jesus." Can you imagine any more powerful, fulfilling, or lasting peace than that which you can receive from the very God who created you?! That is precisely what he wants for every person. It is therefore up to us to do our part in the fulfillment of this promise.

And, one more meaningful quote from the Apostle Paul in this Letter to the Colossians, (citizens of the City of Colossae, then Asia Minor, now Turkey): 3:15, "And may the peace of Christ rein in your hearts, because it is for this that you were called together in one body. Always be thankful!"

The aforementioned quotes, once again, are but a few of the powerful, and substantive uses of the term "Peace" in the Bible which were intended to help the Jewish people, then all the Christians to shoulder the burdens of everyday life, just exactly as we are all trying to do today. So, as you read through the many challenging, brilliant stories of peace, and the wisdom that emanates from a less anxious way of living and thinking, I sincerely believe that you will be richly rewarded, just as I am every day in my readings.

CHAPTER NINE

God's Awesome Story

CHARACTER BUILDING

The art of "Character Building" is complex, challenging, ever-changing, and in the end, when done well, encompasses a multitude of personal, recognizable traits. The positive traits must be built into the very foundation of all those who hope to enjoy a good life, beginning at a very young age. Thereafter, they are added to and refined.

Fortunately, the Holy Bible shares many wonderful examples where character building took on many, varied roles, sometimes with similar outcomes, others not so much.

Both the Old and New Testaments provide some guidance, covering hundreds of years, and very diverse circumstances. I've chosen six powerful examples of individuals who all had major challenges in their respective lives, but who through the development and application of time-honored character traits have been forever memorialized in history.

These individuals are Joseph (son of Jacob, Book of Genesis); David (1 Samuel and 2 Samuel, King); Peter (throughout New Testament); Moses (Genesis); St. Paul (Acts of The Apostles); and Ruth/Naomi (Book of Ruth).

The key characteristics of Character Building, which are components of personal growth that are every bit as important today as they were for centuries include:

- **Integrity**: Acting with honesty, moral principles, and strong ethics. Being truthful, reliable, and consistent in your thoughts, words, and actions.
- **Responsibility**: Taking ownership of your actions and their consequences. Being accountable, fulfilling commitments, and proactive in solving problems.
- **Empathy**: Understanding and sharing the feelings of others, fostering compassionate behavior. Shows kindness, respect, and sensitivity towards other's feelings.
- **Perseverance**: Resilience and willingness to persist in the face of challenges. Embraces failures as learning opportunities.
- **Courage**: Stepping outside your comfort zone to face fears which lead to personal development. Taking risks, standing up for what is right, and facing adversity with bravery.
- **Self-discipline**: Practicing self-control, setting goals, and making consistent efforts to achieve them. Helps you cultivate good habits, manage time effectively, and stay focused on long-term objectives.
- **Generosity**: Being generous with your time, resources, and compassion. Demonstrating a spirit of giving.

To be as successful as one can be in pursuing the development of all, or most of these critical character-building traits is a constant, continual life-long challenge, where self-examination, some peer review, and an awareness of progress or lack thereof is ever-present.

Now, we return to the six Biblical individuals selected earlier in the chapter. I strongly encourage you to read, enjoy, and look carefully for one or more of the character-building traits just discussed in the individuals.

NOTE: Please remember, the primary goal we are attempting to reach is showing that most of the life challenges you face today, were in fact faced, challenged, and for the most part solved or accomplished as illustrated in this incredible book of wisdom, The Holy Bible.

Here we go: (These are all well-documented, true stories).

- Joseph, (son of Jacob in the Book of Genesis): An almost unbelievable set of circumstances led this sheep-herding boy, the youngest of twelve, from being discarded and thrown into a cistern (pit) to die by his jealous brothers, who then rises to be the most powerful and accomplished leader in all of Egypt. You need to read it to believe it, in this gripping story.

- David, (in the two books, 1 Samuel, and 2 Samuel): A fascinating story begins when he was a small boy and was taken under the wing of one of the most powerful prophets in history-Samuel. The story of him facing the Philistine giant, Goliath is, of course famous. But, you need to read the details of how he accomplished his task and see what specific character traits he had to display. Rising ultimately to become King, his story is not without serious moral challenge. Overcoming severe obstacles, he still wrote several of the famous Psalms and dedicated his life to God. A Great read!!

- St. Peter (Begins in the Gospel of Matthew, 4: 18-20): Beginning as a lowly fisherman, he becomes a devoted Apostle of Jesus. But, there is some rocky ground in his future. Even though he says right to Christ's face that he believes He (Jesus) is the Messiah, later he somewhat recants by denying he even knows Him, three times no less, when it is obvious Christ will be brutally crucified, and he doesn't want to share the same fate. The story improves later when Christ reappears after His Resurrection, and Peter is said to be the Rock on which the Christian Church will be built. Don't miss Peter's powerful, convincing, and life-changing speech at the home of Cornelius. It is fantastic!! (Acts of The Apostles).

- Moses (Books of Genesis, and Exodus primarily). Wow. So much to absorb and consider when reviewing the staggering multiplicity of his experiences, beginning as a child floating down the Nile in a wicker basket, only to be rescued by the Pharoh's daughter, all the way to adulthood, leading the enslaved Jewish people out of Egypt, and to the Promised Land of milk and honey. But, whoops, after all that, and literally being God's personal spokesperson to the Israelis, he's not allowed to join the throng of migrants into their new homeland. You'll need to read why, as well as his involvement with The Ten Commandments. Did you know he killed a man? Check to see if he got caught, and what the circumstances were. Lots of incredible history here, and it is thought that he was the primary author of the five books comprising the Jewish Bible, The Pentateuch.

- The Apostle Paul (Acts of The Apostles, beginning Chapter 7:58). Talk about the quintessential about face!! He first appears in the Bible as a brilliant, powerful member of the Jewish elite, the Pharisees, hunting down, imprisoning, and killing newly committed Christians. Then, on his way to Damascus (Syria), to carry out more of his treachery, BAM! His world has a dramatic turn of events, and he is permanently converted. He went on to become the most prolific Christian missionary in history. However, you won't believe all the character-building challenges he faced. A MUST READ, with twists and turns very few people could have survived!

Ruth (The story of Ruth and Naomi, in the Book of Ruth). This is a story of powerful, personal commitment, beginning during a severe famine. Ruth's life is not easy, working in the fields gathering grain. The story highlights themes of loyalty, faithfulness, and God's providence in the lives of ordinary people. Ruth's kindness and thoughtfulness towards Naomi is legendary. You'll also find a connection with King David, but you'll have to look to find it.

Hopefully, you'll see, once you immerse yourself in the stories and lives of these historic Biblical figures, that "Character Building" is very complex, challenging, and somewhat unique in each individual. However, you can see that the foundational aspects which represent these critical traits have been the same for millennia, and so continue today.

See how many other examples you can unearth in your Biblical readings. There are many, many more.

ENJOY!

CHAPTER TEN

God's Awesome Story

CONFLICT RESOLUTION

Resolving conflicts between individuals, groups, and even nations can be either very complex, or relatively simple, depending upon the dynamics of the issues, and individuals involved.

Disagreements arise in our personal lives every day, and exactly how we perceive, and then handle the matters at hand, can result in a positive outcome, or a magnification of the problem.

The Bible literally contains hundreds of conflicts, some of which were resolved peaceably, others failed and resulted in disasters.

Therefore, before we look at specific Biblical examples of Conflict Resolution, we'll need to know what comprises successful approaches.

- **Communication:** Participants must be open, and honest, and express themselves clearly;

- **Active Listening:** Attentively hear and understand the other person's point of view, without interrupting or judging;
- **Empathy and Understanding:** It is very important to understand the other person's needs and perspectives. When done, this will create a sense of connectedness;
- **Collaboration:** A cooperative and collaborative approach is important for success when negotiating. Parties should be able to share, and find mutually beneficial solutions;
- **Problem Solving:** It is critical to understand the underlying issues, and focus on problem-solving, rather than blaming each other. Evaluate the pros and cons, and attempt to find a middle ground;
- **Compromise and Flexibility:** Willingness to be flexible is essential to resolving conflicts. It may not be that everyone is satisfied with the result, but a mediated outcome is certainly better than a continuation of the conflict.
- **Respect and Fairness:** Understand and respect the other party's opinions, boundaries, and rights, which will show a willingness on your part to end a possible stalemate.
- **Patience and Emotional Control:** Basically, these should be in capital letters, because they are not only essential to a positive outcome, but they are frequently the cause for an eruption of personal anxieties, but unless kept in check, it will be a sure cause for failure.

Let us now look at some interesting Biblical conflict resolutions, some of which are thousands of years old, but every bit as up-to-date as other recommended solutions.

- Abraham and Lot (Genesis 13). Abraham was Lot's uncle, and they found themselves in a conflict over having their herds share the same land for grazing, and there was insufficient food for the animals of the combined herds. Abraham came up with a simple, practical, and successful suggestion. He offered Lot one of two options: "You take the land over there, I'll take the land over here. Or, you can reverse it, and I'll take the land you choose to reject".

In today's vernacular, we call this a "Chinese Option", which goes like this: assuming there is a disagreement between two parties on sharing, say a cherry pie, the fair way to do it says the first person cuts the pie, the other has the first choice to select a piece. Obviously, the person cutting the pie will attempt to cut it as perfectly even as possible, since he will receive only what is left.

- Gospel of St. Matthew (5:23-25). There are actually two very interesting stories here that depict conflict resolution. One has to do with conflict with a family member (brother), the other with a conflict that is headed to court…with great advice as to how to avoid an adverse outcome. Be sure not to miss the approach taken here.

- Gospel of St. Matthew (18: 15-17). Once again, this is an illustration of a conflict with a brother, who represents another community member. This resolution has several critical steps in an attempt to resolve the matter and is very illustrative of conflicts we see every day in our lives. The key is in the approach!!

- Letter of Paul to the Ephesians; (4:31). "Any bitterness or bad temper or anger or shouting or abuse must be far removed from you, as must every kind of malice". Here Paul is profoundly setting the stage for conflicts that have arisen in the new Ephesian congregation, which were frequent between the Jews, Gentiles, and newly converted Christians. He is obviously letting there be no doubt about these human, emotional elements that contribute to a continuation of conflict.

- Paul's Letter to the Philippians; (4:2-3). Here is yet another of the many churches Paul's ministry has developed. As any nascent organization would expect, especially one with such profound religious roots, there was conflict. Here, Paul seeks a resolution between two, quarreling women: "I urge Euodia, and I urge Syntyche to come to an agreement with each other in the name of the Lord! And I ask you, Syzygal, really to be a "partner" and help them.

  Here Paul is taking a twofold approach: first, he is asking the ladies involved to settle the matter between themselves, with some spiritual help. He then requests the intercession of a third party for assistance. What Paul is saying, the conflict must be resolved, and here are my suggestions!

As you go through the many stories of the Bible, you will be able to literally find hundreds of examples of conflict resolution. The Old Testament is filled with conflicts between cities, and cultures. Too often the resolution, as today, resulted in tens of thousands of deaths. The New Testament, with the arrival of Jesus, the Prince of Peace, opens a whole new, exciting series of dramatic demonstrations, discussions, and brilliant wisdom to help us understand each other, and gives us a very clear and descriptive pathway toward "conflict resolution." Once you get involved in the beauty, and power of The Word, it will change your life for the better!

CHAPTER ELEVEN

God's Awesome Story

WISDOM

Many people confuse wisdom with raw intelligence. The fact is you can have a very high IQ, but be seriously lacking in wisdom.

So, exactly what is wisdom? Is it acquired or innate (IQ)? How exactly do you acquire it, therefore, if you are not born with it?

Basically, wisdom is a fascinating and complex combination of knowledge, experience, and insight, and then extends all that which has been accumulated in these efforts/undertakings towards wise application in real-life circumstances. It enhances sound judgement and shows good discernment (making good decisions on somewhat difficult problems), frequently under stressful conditions.

Wisdom allows us to go beyond the "obvious", helping to benefit both ourselves and others. Wisdom is constantly evolving, as we encounter multiple new life experiences from which we gain additional insights. As well, it helps us to navigate through life with grace, compassion, and a sense of fairness and purpose.

Wisdom more typically is directly associated with human values, human pursuits, and human fulfillment. That's why; when acquired and accurately developed and applied it is greatly cherished.

Now, let's turn to the primary theme of this book, and ask what does the Bible have to do with wisdom? Also, what relationship does wisdom have with spirituality or faith? Or, is there a connection?

Before we examine five primary and brilliant sources of wisdom in the Bible, let's pause for a moment and consider the following quote: **"Our findings show that spirituality is significantly associated with better mental health, well-being, and may add to an individual's overall wisdom"**. This is from Dr. Dilsp V. Jeste, MD, Center of Health and Aging, and Distinguished Professor of Psychiatry and Neurosciences, UC San Diego School of Medicine.

Aha, this may therefore take "wisdom" to an additional dimension in our study.

Following are some of the Wisdom Books, as described in the Bible, most of which are widely known and quoted frequently at least in some form:

- Proverbs
- Psalms
- Job
- Sirach
- Ecclesiastes

Book of Proverbs

This book of multiple insights into life is generally attributed to King Solomon in the Old Testament. Here we find a collection of wise sayings and teachings that provide guidance for living a virtuous and fulfilling life. It contains a wide range of topics including wisdom, morality, relationships, work ethics, family, and practical advice on certain aspects of daily life. It resonates with people of different cultures and backgrounds. It encourages the pursuit of virtues such as honesty, humility, and kindness.

Additionally, it emphasizes the importance of seeking knowledge and understanding and states that wisdom is more important than material possessions. Finally, it promotes discernment and critical thinking, encouraging readers to carefully consider their choices and actions in life.

Book of Psalms

This book holds immense importance and significance in both religious and literary contexts. It is a collection of poetic hymns and prayers attributed to various authors, a prominent one being King David. They express a wide range of emotions, including joy, sorrow, gratitude, fear, and hope, and make it all relevant to people throughout history.

The Psalms, moreover, serve as a source of wisdom, and guidance. Many psalms reflect on the qualities of God, His faithfulness, and justice. Also, they provide insights into human nature, offering comfort and encouragement in times of distress, and guidance for righteous living. They promote trust, forgiveness, and perseverance.

There are a total of 150 psalms in the book, some at greater length than others. The Book of Psalms is meant to be read patiently, with a contemplative mindset, just as the Book of Proverbs should similarly be approached, and only in small segments, not all at once.

Book of Job

Essentially, in this incomparable writing the overall theme can be summarized as the problem of human suffering, and the search for meaning in the face of adversity. Further, it explores profound questions about the nature of God, and the existence of evil, along with a particularly brilliant handling of the human response to suffering as seen not only through Job's eyes, who is the unfortunate recipient of bad tidings and events, but through several other key players in the drama.

The book raises profound questions that in part, we face in everyday life, ourselves, which helps make the story all the more relevant. It emphasizes that suffering is not necessarily a punishment for sin, but can be part of the human experience, even for the righteous!

The writing style, content, and attention to detail in a unique and very readable format make this "wisdom book" one you'll want to read multiple times. And in the end, you'll more than likely be rewarded with the proverbial, "patience of Job"!

Book of Ecclesiastes

Written by an anonymous author who referred to himself as The Teacher, around 970 BCE (Before Current Era, or Before Christ BC), reflects the meaning and purpose of life. This book presents a unique perspective on the human experience and pursuit of happiness. This is where the term "vanity of vanities, all is vanity" comes from. The author explores a search for meaning, such as wisdom, pleasure, and wealth, only to find they all come up short of his expectations. The book warns about placing too much importance on earthly pleasures and possessions, as they will ultimately fail to provide lasting satisfaction or true fulfillment.

Book of Sirach

The Book of Sirach is also known as The Book of Ecclesiasticus. The author provides a wisdom guide for moral and practical living, including valuable insights for individuals and communities, alike. He addresses topics and offers guidance on the value of friendship, the value and importance of wisdom, the role of parents and children, the pursuit of justice, and the significance of charity.

The author emphasizes the importance of observing religious laws, and traditions. Preserving the moral integrity of the individual and community is primary to living a righteous life.

The Book of Sirach is beautifully written, so as to provide a maximum level of insight and enjoyment.

Therefore, the value and impact of these incredible books of wisdom cannot be overstated. In a brief recapitulation, by reading these books you will enjoy in-depth discussions, the validity of which is borne out over centuries of living, and is constantly evolving:

- Insight into the human condition
- Human needs resolution
- Good decision-making and discernment
- Interpersonal relations with family and community
- Emphasis on fairness, emotional, and moral balance
- Work ethics
- Family
- Patience
- Perseverance
- Encouragement in times of stress
- Better understanding and acceptance of yourself

Obviously, these books are a MUST read!

CHAPTER TWELVE

God's Awesome Story

JUDGEMENT

Judgement. There is good judgement and bad judgement. When and how will you know which is being executed at any given point in time, since just waiting for the outcome is not a preferred choice? The judgement may be one you are exercising, or, it may be that which someone else is proposing which may adversely impact you.

But, how do you tell? What criteria do you use to ensure a positive outcome? The judgement you are exercising may be as simple as which bill to pay next out of a limited income that month. Or, it may be as serious as choosing a partner for life. Or, it may be a moral judgement that won't be measured in a legalistic framework, but by religious and cultural standards.

Therefore, recognizing and exercising the best judgement, at the right time and place, under varying circumstances is not only necessary but can be critical to your well-being.

So, let's examine some time-proven steps towards understanding a protocol for determining and understanding good judgment, either from you or a third party:

- First, perform a critical thinking analysis, this requires an objective, analytical approach;
- Utilize your knowledge and experiences in past or similar situations;
- Omit the emotional pull that may be adversely affecting your judgement;
- Consider your values and ethics, and how they will be impacted;
- When possible exercise time and patience so as not to be rushed to judgement;
- Seek outside opinions to add to, or narrow your choices;
- And, learn from your mistakes (and by observing the mistakes of others).

In today's world, with our minds and senses being constantly bombarded by social media, it is increasingly critical to separate the true facts from either fake or exaggerated information. A good judgement also dictates what information flow you subject yourself to, and how you react to varying opinions on the same subject (such as the current controversies over illegal immigration, or abortion).

Therefore, somehow, somewhere, by some means there must be some insight into a foundation for good judgement since people have existed on this earth for tens of thousands of years. And, fortunately, yes, there are some time-proven guidelines. In fact, there are dozens in our "self-help book", The Holy Bible.

Let's take a look at some of the examples of judgement that emanate from scripture:

- Gospel of Matthew: Chapter 7:1-5; "Do not judge, and you will not be judged, because the judgements you give are the judgements you will get, and the standard you use will be the standard for you".
- Gospel of Luke: Chapter 6:37; " Forgive, and you will be forgiven".
- You can't be any more straight-forward than that! To me, it is compatible with the Second Commandment, "Love thy neighbor as thyself." Under both circumstances, when you are exercising judgement on a particular issue, when either or both these statements are considered, the likelihood of a good outcome is certainly enhanced.
- Another wise and powerful description of judgement is found in 1 Peter, Chapter 4:17; "The time has come for the judgement to begin at the household of God, and if it begins with us, what will be the end for those who refuse to believe God's gospel?"
- Finally, this quote from St. Paul's Letter to the people of Corinth, Greece, 2000 years ago, which still bears solid advice today: 2 Corinthians, Chapter 5:10; "For at the judgement seat of Christ, we are all seen for what we are, so that each of us may receive what he has deserved in the body, matched to whatever he has done, good or bad."

Of course, the quintessential guidepost for exercising and understanding good judgement is wrapped up in the Ten Commandments.

Yes, these were first recorded in our most famous Scriptures, (Genesis, and Exodus, then repeated in the New Testament), but remember, they were handed down to the Jewish people, then ultimately to all mankind, not only as religious and cultural directives, but personal, legal, commitments as well.

As a reminder, here they are: (Note: Can you pick out the Spiritual, Cultural, and Legal influences?):

- One: You shall love the Lord thy God with all your heart, all your soul, and all your mind;
- Two: Love your neighbor as yourself;
- Three: Do not take the name of the Lord in vain;
- Four: Remember to keep holy the Sabbath day;
- Five: Honor your father and mother;
- Six: Do not kill;
- Seven: Do not steal;
- Eight: Do not commit adultery;
- Nine: Do not covet (be envious of) your neighbor's wife or possessions:
- Ten: Do not bear false witness against your neighbor.

Why have I included the Ten Commandments in a chapter on "Judgement"? Simple. Should you exercise judgement that violates any or all of the above, you will most assuredly come under the judgement of either God, your husband or wife, your neighbor, or the local court system, and pay the requisite price.

The moral of the story: Know what good judgement is, and exercise it freely.

Now, enjoy reading and searching the Bible for literally hundreds of additional examples of judgement both good and bad!

CHAPTER THIRTEEN

God's Awesome Story

FORGIVENESS

Forgiveness is unquestionably one of the most difficult human emotions we need to express, and its right up there with "Love thy neighbor as thy self" in terms of the degree of difficulty. Both require a total personal commitment to expunge, or purify ourselves of personal hurts, animosity, and prejudices. Whew! That's a lot to ask of ourselves!!

Yet, unless both are practiced with an open heart and sincerity, neither will accomplish the intended goal.

Let's take a closer look at the types, or origins of forgiveness which will hopefully better prepare us whenever a situation arises that requires us to take such an action.

- Personal forgiveness relates directly to a situation generally with one other person, whom we feel has hurt or wronged us. Letting go of the memory of the event that caused the emotional distress, as well as the anger and resentment built up is certainly a necessary and helpful prerequisite.

- Interpersonal forgiveness involves taking a positive step towards reducing the angst that exists between you and several others. This is necessary to repair the relationship, and restore trust.

- Self-forgiveness. Aha. This is a unique form of forgiveness, and to be successful often needs an effective catharsis, or cleansing of mistakes, regrets, of personal failures. By taking this action in a timely manner, you can avoid damaging your own emotional stability. Frequently people are much harder on themselves than they are on others, primarily because their expectations of themselves fall short when reality sets in. Setting realistic goals and logical or common sense criteria for measuring your progress is generally most helpful.

- Conditional forgiveness can be given when only certain portions of expectations of a reconciliation have been completed. In other words, more to come!

- Collective forgiveness can cover an entire community or even a country for past wrong-doings, such as historical injustices. A classic example of this on an enormous scale was the development and deployment of the Marshall Plan after World War II. Even though Germany was the central cause of the deaths of millions of people, the United States and some of its allies invested tens of billions of dollars to help Germany and other Eastern European countries to reindustrialize and get back on an economic and sustainable foundation.

Now, once again it's fascinating when we search for examples of the origin of forgiveness on many different levels, we can return to The Scriptures.

- There are few better or more articulate examples of personal forgiveness than in the Parable of The Prodigal Son, found in Luke, Chapter 15: 15-32. This is a great story! Can you imagine being the father in this drama, and seeing his miscreant son coming back to him, stumbling down the road, after blowing his inheritance, and living a life of debauchery? But, what a finish!! Also, pay particular attention to the lesson of the elder son. This is a classic to be read several times over.

  Another powerful example of personal forgiveness is represented in the story of the "woman caught in adultery", John: 8: 1-11. Be sure to pay attention to Christ writing in the sand. What do you think He is writing, and why does it have such an impact on the men who are watching?

- An example of conditional forgiveness can be found throughout the Old Testament, where god, who has made a covenant with the Jewish people to make them the chosen ones, reminds them that His forgiveness is conditioned upon their commitment to live by His commandments, the Ten Commandments to be exact, and stop making idols to worship. This turns out to be a very hard lesson to learn!

- Collective forgiveness is very, very powerfully illustrated in many of The Scriptures. Try this one for openers, if you can possibly imagine: Jesus Christ, the very Son of God, willingly accepts humiliation, beatings, suffering, crucifixion, and death to do what…forgive ALL sinners for engaging in unacceptable behavior by themselves, and with others! An unbelievable, almost unbearable story of forgiveness, that has (and continues to do so) changed billions of lives. This story is told, and re-told in all the four Gospel accounts of Matthew, Mark, Luke, and John. When you read the various accounts of this "collective forgiveness", I suggest you sit quietly by yourself and reflect on the incredible unselfishness and love that is herein depicted. It...is...life...changing.

One other example of collective forgiveness is vividly shown by Stephen, while he is being stoned to death for his powerful Christian testimony. Found in the Book of Acts of The Apostles, Chapter 7: 54-60. This, too, is an example of forgiveness on a whole new level.

- Finally, self-forgiveness, as has been discussed, can be extraordinarily difficult. For one reason, you know exactly what you did, when you did it, but possibly not why you did it.

- It is my observation that the two following examples fit into this category.

- First, we find St. Peter originally recognizing Christ as the Messiah when asked by Jesus, himself. Then, on three separate occasions later, he denies he even knows Christ. In the end, he regains his senses and becomes a powerful, influential "rock" of the Christian faith. That had to have required substantial and successful self-examination. You'll find this played out over several chapters in the New Testament.

There is one other "aha" moment in the Gospel of John, Chapter 20:24-29. This is when Thomas, one of the twelve Apostles realizes his grievous error in doubting that Christ has in fact returned from the dead, and comments, "My Lord and my God". Obviously, the "doubting Thomas" had a personal reconciliation that was a life changer for him.

The origin of "things" has always been of a particular fascination for me. Where did something come from? Why? Who was involved? Was it nature at work? Was it purely physical, metaphysical, or spiritual?

After spending much time completely immersed in the Bible, hundreds of my lifelong questions have found not only the origin but also the answers I was seeking.

So, keep reading, keep searching, keep enjoying the incomparable Bible.

CHAPTER FOURTEEN

God's Awesome Story

COMPASSION

Compassion. A word certainly familiar to all of us, but what does it really mean, and how many variations are there to this powerful human emotion?

Quite frankly, you may be surprised as to the multiple ways to express this emotion. Therefore, let's review several:

- Familial compassion is exercised within your own family. A brother, sister, or parent is hurting in some way, be it emotionally or physically. Your compassion propels you to take action to help alleviate the pain:

- Familiar compassion shows concern for friends or relatives;

- Stranger compassion seems obvious, and even though you may not know the person with whom you are showing this particular kindness, they will in all likelihood be extremely appreciative. In this particular case, the person receiving your compassionate response to their need may not have requested it, but nonetheless will more than likely welcome it.

Incidentally, later in this book, there is a very powerful illustration of this type of compassion in a Biblical parable and some of you may already be guessing which one it is!

There are other ways to view and define compassion, as well, and those are listed below. Understandably, compassion is often confused with empathy. They are slightly different in that compassion requires action, whereas empathy can simply be a verbal action.

- Spiritual compassion relates to the dignity and worth of others, to the point where you may even wish to participate or assist them in their journey;
- Cognitive compassion recognizes suffering through a statistical or intellectual lens. An example would be listening to a friend describe a particular problem or pain they are currently experiencing, and using your own background to help analyze and offer a solution to mitigate the situation.
- Practical compassion is just as it sounds. You see a problem or someone suffering, and you offer a practical solution for their benefit. Remember, compassion requires some overt action on your part.
- Self-compassion helps you to realize the pain or suffering being inflicted upon yourself. An example of this would be vocational burnout. Action is required.
- Finally, there is universal compassion wherein a person expresses a sensitivity towards all human beings, animals, and the environment. Obviously, in this case, taking action to alleviate the pain and suffering must be realistic, and

taken in small, incremental steps if there is to be any sense of satisfaction or accomplishment.

Now that we've observed the many varied types of compassion, there are few books or reference materials that offer such an incredible and comprehensive series of life examples as The Holy Bible.

Stay with me on this one, because you are in for a fascinating, unique, and educational journey.

- One of the most popular, and certainly a favorite of mine, is the Parable of The Good Samaritan, found in Luke; Chapter 10: 25-37. To best understand this almost incomparable act of compassion, you need to pay close attention to the players involved. The lawyer who initiated the question to Jesus is a member of the ruling Jewish community. The injured man is anonymous. The Levite who first passes by is a member of the ruling elite, as well. The priest who ignores the beaten and suffering victim is a member of the local religious society.

    Now comes the interesting part. The "Good Samaritan" who shows such meaningful compassion is a part of the sect that Jews disregard as being worthy to be included in their culture. The more you read and dissect the component parts of this story, the more powerful it becomes! (If you've never read the Bible and this story is new to you, the ending will have special meaning).

Next, the unequalled examples of compassion come from Jesus, himself. Following are just a few, so I strongly recommend you search dozens more throughout The Scriptures:

- Luke 17: 11-19. Jesus heals ten lepers who are suffering from this terrible, and ultimately fatal skin disease;

- Mark 1: 40-42. Another man suffering from a skin disease pleads, on his knees, for Jesus to cure him, saying, "If you are willing, you can cleanse me," and of course, Jesus does exactly that. What a show of faith, and compassion!

- Luke 7: 11-15 Read the story of Jesus bringing back to life a man, who was the only son of his widowed mother, and who had recently died. This is in the town of Nain, and Jesus's compassion is clearly life-changing;

- John 19: 26-27 Even though Jesus was just moments from death, he looked down at his suffering mother, and asked that she be taken care of. Touching, powerful, beautiful.

- In several instances in the Old Testament, God instructs the Jewish people and their leaders to "act with compassionate hearts, kindness, humility, meekness, and patience". Search for these examples, particularly in Genesis, Exodus, Deuteronomy, Job, Isaiah, Jeremiah, and many others. It is fabulous reading, and you'll find it personally rewarding'

- Matthew 20: 29-34. Jesus is deeply moved with pity and compassion by two blind men, whereupon he gives them their sight.

- Matthew 15: 32-39, and Matthew 14: 13-21. Here, Jesus uses His divine powers in fulfilling two huge acts of compassion and kindness by feeding 4,000 and 5000 of His followers, respectively. This begins when it states "Jesus as He stepped ashore, He saw a large crowd, and He took pity on them, and healed their sick". He then fed them all!

- Finally, in Matthew 18: 21-35 you'll find another parable with which you will more than likely relate in your own life. It is the Parable of the Unforgiving Servant. Most of us have witnessed this behavior firsthand.

These are but a few of the examples, why the Biblical stories are so meaningful. You don't build a building without a blueprint, so why try to go through life without instructions which have been tested, and minted over thousands of years?!

Compassion, besides being a very powerful personal emotion, can be a life-changing event, both for the giver, as well as the recipient. Take action. Share it freely!

CHAPTER FIFTEEN

God's Awesome Story

FAITH

Faith is something so intangible, yet so very real that we cannot ignore it. Ostensibly, it is mentioned with reference to religion, connected with spirituality. However, when you stop and think about it, you use faith in everyday life so frequently that you really don't give it consideration.

For example, have you used Google Maps or their navigational system lately to get to your destination? You had faith in the professionalism and accuracy of their mapping platform, and so followed it exactly as you had been directed. In the vast majority of cases, there was a positive outcome to having this faith.

There are, of course, dozens more experiences you have wherein faith in the outcome is not only hopeful but expected. The elevator you take performs as it should. You expect your children to return home safely from school, and they do. The airliner you are on takes off and lands safely at your intended destination.

All these examples begin with a faith you have either predetermined or experienced in the past. In the expression, "someone shook my faith", in an event or another person, illustrates that faith IS A PRECURSOR, something that happens in the beginning, with the outcome unknown until it happens.

So, how does faith become relevant in your life? More than likely you are convinced that a future event will occur as expected either from something you read, heard, or experienced yourself. In the New Testament, there is a very interesting definition of "faith" in the Book of Hebrews. Chapter 11: 1-2; "Only faith can guarantee the blessings that we hope for, or prove the existence of realities that are unseen. It is for their faith that our ancestors are acknowledged. It is by faith that we understand that the ages were created by a word from God **so that from the invisible the visible world came to be**".

This is very important now, so stick with me. This is getting good! When reading the Bible, you will quickly realize that faith plays a significant role. Many people become disillusioned or misguided that they are predisposed to the erroneous assumption that "faith in God" is something totally intangible, and esoteric that it is difficult to get your arms around it.

However, let's take a close look at the Biblical examples of how faith became reality, just as in the examples above with Google Maps, and Elevator.

In the Book of Exodus, it was faith turned into a reality that helped Moses understand his role in gathering, directing, and leading thousands of Jewish people safely through the Red Sea (which in turn drowned all the Pharoh's army who were in hot pursuit), and into the Promised Land.

It was faith turned into reality by famous Old Testament Prophets such as Isaiah, and Daniel who had faith centuries earlier that Jesus Christ was to be born as the Messiah the Jewish people longed for, and who would change millions of lives, forever. See the following examples of their faith:

- Isaiah 7:14, "Therefore, the Lord Himself will give you a sign: The virgin will conceive and give birth to a son, and will call him Immanuel" (meaning God is with us). So yes, this actually happened 700 years later, and it all began with faith.
- Isaiah's faith went further in 9:6, "For to us a child is born, to us a son is given, and the government will be on his shoulders. And He will be called wonderful counselor, Mighty God, Everlasting Father, and Prince of Peace". Isaiah finally shares yet a most powerful faith in Chapter 53: "He will be a suffering servant who bears the sins of others". This, also, is an example of faith turning into fact, since historical records prove his predictions and help justify his faith.

As well, this faith and incredible outcome turn out to be the very cornerstone of the Christian faith as represented throughout The New Testament.

In the Book of Daniel, we find yet one more accurate and well-deserved expression of faith that became reality. 7:13-14 "In my vision at night I looked, and there before me was one like a son of man, coming with the clouds of heaven. He approached the Ancient of Days and was led in His presence. He was given authority, glory, and sovereign power over all nations, and people of every language worshiped Him. **His dominion is an everlasting dominion that will not pass away, and His Kingdom is one that will never be destroyed".** This faith, too, has been proven to be undaunted.

Fortunately, the Bible is loaded with great "faith turned into reality" examples, or we might say "faith fulfilled". Following is a brief peek at what is in store for you as you dig more deeply into this fabulous Book:

- One of the most incredible acts of faith is described in Genesis, Chapter 22: 1-19. God challenges Abraham, the very father of the nation of Israel, to prove his faith by sacrificing his only son, putting him to death. But, what happens is an astonishing and everlasting act of faith. You must read it to believe it!

- In Matthew, 9: 20-22, and repeated in Mark 5: 25-34, and Luke 8: 43-48, a woman who has a history of bleeding reached out when Jesus was walking by, and said if I can just touch his garment, I can be healed. Jesus acknowledged her powerful faith and fulfilled her wish.

- In yet another act of faith turned into reality, this time not by dreaming (Daniel), nor physical sacrifice (Abraham), nor by touching Jesus's cloak, but by merely having faith that Jesus could cure one of his most valuable men, a Centurion officer sent a messenger to Jesus, and the cure was done from a distance. Now THAT is faith, and Jesus and the Centurian acknowledged it as well.

Interestingly, there is at least one recognizable lack of faith that eventually had a positive lesson (not counting the "doubting Thomas episode, mentioned earlier). It is described in Matthew, 14: 22-33, and our main character is once again, Peter. In a most unusual display of His Divinity, Jesus is walking on water, approaching the disciples' boat. Peter decides to meet Jesus, steps out of the boat, and for a brief period, he too is walking on water.

Whereupon, he begins to sink, and Christ remarks, "Oh ye of little faith".

So, we see, in the end, that faith does in fact have tangible, factual, results even though it begins with a thought, a hope, and a dream.

And, for Christians, the faith that Christ has died for our sins **(fact)**, and that we have an opportunity for everlasting life with Him, is faith that will come to fruition.

KEEP THE FAITH

CHAPTER SIXTEEN

God's Awesome Story

CHOOSING A MENTOR

Mentoring can be viewed from two perspectives: the person doing the mentoring, (Mentor), and the recipient, (Mentee).

First, let's discuss your search for a person who can help you reach higher levels of achievement, whatever your goals may be. Precisely what criteria do you use prior to your selection process? Are you interested in a mentor for vocational advancement, or for personal growth, or both? What exactly do you hope to achieve?

Once you've created your "mentor wish list", the next challenge is where to find that person. But, before we get ahead of ourselves, let's examine our preferred requirements, and set a foundation.

Now, the following list may seem rather onerous, but nonetheless, it contains many of the critical characteristics of a good mentor, with whom you expect to not only develop personally and professionally but with whom you will be relying on for serious growth.

The following is what you would hope for and expect from this person:

- An interpersonal relationship to be built on mutual respect, and trust
- Guidance through uncharted territories
- Leadership on multiple levels
- Strength and wisdom to get through the most challenging and difficult problems
- Support and direction when you are either faltering or anticipating a crisis
- Confidence in problem-solving, since as you grow, problems have a way of increasing as well. Be sure to address them early!
- Personal growth and development towards a vocation or the ability to deal with life's problems
- Shows an understanding and concern for your needs and goals, and gives appropriate and relevant directives and insight into their respective requirements
- Creates procedures for measuring results on an ongoing basis

Whew. Those are all very important, so keep in mind that the mentor/mentee relationship is a collaborative journey, which will hopefully include the following, as well:

- Sharing a safe space to clearly express thoughts
- Fosters self-awareness
- Is realistic in creating milestones for developmental targets
- Is a good listener

- And your relationship, which will be built on mutual respect, will always be completely transparent

Now, as you go over these long lists, you may say it is unrealistic to expect all of those characteristics from one person, and you may be right…partially.

To give an analogy, all the above may be likened to a good, well-diversified diet. You take from certain food groups and know instinctively what will help you experience good health, and hopefully improve your longevity. However, you will soon find out that too much, or too little of certain foods is not only not in your best interest, but may be the reverse of your expectations.

Only you will know the effects of your choices, and so it is with choosing a good mentor relationship. In other words, you need to keep a close monitor to measure achievement levels as you reach each agreed-upon milestone.

Now, all that notwithstanding, fortunately for you and me there is a powerful, all-knowing, loving "Life Mentor" available to us all, and yes, His name is Jesus Christ.

What would you look for from a "Life Mentor"? Support? Encouragement? Love? Rules? Answers? Problem-solving? Respect? Proven life concepts? And most likely, someone who is emotionally strong, wise, and whom you can look up to.

As you initiate your "Life Mentor" search, I suggest you begin by reading at least one of the New Testament Gospels, say either Matthew or John. In your Study Bible, check out the Reading Guide and the introduction prior to the actual text, as they will help you better understand and position the rich and fascinating information you are about to read.

The story of the "Life Mentor" is described in great detail, and is so unique as to never before nor since has it been replicated.

But, here is the key. How did He mentor? With whom were His endless capabilities shared? What were some of the outcomes?

When you were just an infant, you had no mobility. Soon you learned to crawl, then stand and walk, then run. It was a necessary progression to become as mobile as you had hoped so that your ability to accomplish many more goals would come to fruition, and it all came in stages.

In the early stages of your exploring Christ as a "Life Mentor", it is important to understand who He is, where He came from, what His goals were for His mentees (you and I), and overall what did He accomplish. (Spoiler Alert: His mentorship continues to this day and has successfully influenced billions; yes that's billions with a "b" of people over the past 2,000 years).

Why has He been so successful, and is He the one for you? The answers to these two questions are illustrated in brilliant, understandable, life-changing detail in the New Testament. I have been particularly moved by the four Gospels of Matthew, Mark, Luke, and John. As well as The Acts of The Apostles, The Letters of Apostle Paul, and others (loved James Letter), are absolutely great, not only from a historical perspective but for the depth of their explaining spirituality.

As you enjoy reading through these Scriptures, pay close attention to why Christ's mentorship was, and remains so very unique, and successful.

First, He was totally and completely unselfish. His primary goals were to honor His Father (God), explain what is expected of your life and actions, guide you through all life's obstacles, suffer for you to have your many indiscretions forgiven, and then die for you to ultimately join Him in great joy for all eternity.

Whew! Wow!! Not too many other "Life Mentors" you know could make and fulfill as well as support your entire life in such a way as to achieve that outcome!

Here are but a few of His mentoring characteristics:

- He was revolutionary in that He concentrated on the hearts, minds, and souls of people, rather than social status and material possessions.
- He preached and shared Love, Compassion, and Forgiveness.
- He inspired and empowered His disciples, embracing their own potential to grow personally and spiritually.
- He rewarded caring and doing good for others, particularly the poor, and indigent.
- He led by example and exercised great patience and selflessness.
- He used His divine power to perform many miracles, which were witnessed and authenticated by thousands.
- And, finally, He required personal discipline, respect, and faith in the rules He and His Father set down The Ten Commandments.

So, if you want an incomparable "Life Mentor", here He is, and He is free, available, and anxious for you to step forward and commit to a life-changing relationship.

CHAPTER SEVENTEEN

God's Awesome Story

"LIFE MENTOR'S WISDOM AND ADVICE"

Now, the "Life Mentor" we have been discussing is similar in some ways to an athletic coach you may have had in school.

First of all, the coach wouldn't be in his or her position if they weren't qualified to help you learn, improve, better yourself, and contribute to an overall effort. Our "Life Mentor" is even much more powerful and special in so many ways.

In our case, the mentor is Jesus Christ. He teaches, guides, directs, and supports and forgives, on many different levels to ensure our success in life. Sometimes, He is very straight-forward and direct, other times He tells a story with a very specific message for a critical life lesson.

Before we inspect some of these fascinating and instructional stories, called parables, let's look at a commitment to us that He makes in Matthew, Chapter 6: 25-32. "I am telling you not to worry about your life and what you are to eat, nor about your body and what you are to wear. Surely life is more important than food, and the body more than clothing. Look at the birds in the sky. They do not sow or reap or gather into barns, yet your Heavenly Father feeds them. **Are you not worth much more than they are?** Can any of you, however much you worry, add one single day to your span of life? Set your hearts on His Kingdom first, and on God's saving justice, and all these things will be given to you as well."

How about THAT for a "Life Mentor" commitment to you!

As previously mentioned, sometimes He is very direct, as in John 14:15, "If you love me, you will keep my Commandments". Then, throughout the four Gospels, He teaches more indirectly through thought-provoking stories or parables.

Here we'll examine several of the most popular:

- Have you ever felt lost, as in nobody really cares about you, and in fact, you're not even convinced, sometimes, of the direction you're headed in life?

    Well, there is an excellent and most applicable parable that would very much be of interest to you. It's called The Parable of the Lost Sheep. In the story, only one sheep out of a hundred gets lost from the herd, but you watch closely how vital and important that one sheep is (you!), and how God as the all-caring Shepherd goes out of His way to rescue the wandering sheep. This is a very reassuring parable. Luke 15: 3-7.

- Did you ever get to the point where you feel it might be too late for you to believe and trust in God? In other words, does He operate on a time limit? The Parable of The Workers in the Vineyard clearly shows that not only are you always welcome, and in God's heart and mind, but it is never too late to ask for His forgiveness and Grace. He is a loving

Father and is on your side in every part of life, but you must do your part as well. As the last worker in the field realized, you must show up, and do what is expected of you and you will be richly rewarded.

- Have you been "down and out", depressed, and feeling totally helpless, and alone? That must have been how the victim of a severe beating, and robbery must have felt in The Parable of the Good Samaritan. In discussing this parable, it is customary to emphasize only The Good Samaritan. But, the victim was in a desperate condition and needed serious care and love to survive, and fully recover. In this example, his needs were initially ignored by people you would ordinarily think would be the first to step in and help. But, they didn't, which is similar to real life!

- However, thanks to the compassion, caring, and love of not only the Good Samaritan but don't forget the commitment by the Innkeeper, too. Incredible story. Luke 10: 25-37.

- Do you ever find yourself afraid and anxious about tomorrow? Is your tendency to gather everything you can, create as big a nest egg as possible, and continue growing it as much as possible? In other words, make sure you are in charge of your future.

- Well, similarly there is a very prophetic parable called The Rich Fool. Materialism and volume consumed his efforts, wherein he fully expected to enjoy these accumulated treasures for a long time, even the rest of his life. Until… he didn't.

  God's offerings and gifts are different than the Rich Fool's, and what seems obvious may surprise you. Read it to find out in Luke 12: 16-31.

- Have you ever felt like you really screwed up in life (haven't we all!), and said to yourself, if I only had it to do all over again, I would do things differently? In fact, you'd give anything to have the proverbial slate wiped clean.

    Well, along comes the Parable of The Prodigal Son, which has been briefly alluded to earlier in this book.

    However, here are some reminders. The thrill of getting something for nothing is always an unexpected delight. It is frequently followed by an embarrassing squandering of your ill-gotten booty, since you did no work, nor put forth any effort to attain it. In the simplest, you didn't earn it, so you don't appreciate it.

    What if…you were given a second chance? Or, maybe even multiple "second chances"? Well, it is God's promise, through His Son Jesus Christ, that this can come about. Notice I say "can", since the forgiveness illustrated in this parable once again is a two-way street.

    Note how penitent the younger son is. That is a requirement for you, too. So, read and enjoy the multiple lessons shared in this classic parable. Luke 15: 12-32.

- In this vast world, it is sometimes easy to feel small and insignificant. Well, there is a very interesting parable that puts that feeling completely to bed. It's The Parable of the Mustard Seed.

    In yet another unique and educational story, Christ uses the vastness and endless power of Heaven to help us understand that not only are we part of something much, much larger, but we are a very important component part of His system.

    Yes, we may seem small, but Christ tells us that with the strength of faith, we can accomplish virtually anything. Now, that's not a faith that is only partial, hesitant, or easily dissipated when challenged. It is firm, committed, strong, and loving.

OK, got that? Then let's go out and do our part to change and improve the world, through His Grace, wisdom, and Divine Will.

- Hey, would you like to know where you fit in with relation to what I believe is the most all-encompassing, "where am I" parable? Well, just open your Bible to The Parable of the Sower, and it will quickly become evident.

  In this most unique and challenging "Biblical Indexing", Christ describes in very understandable and clear detail how we humans can look at ourselves in the mirror, and take inventory of just how we are living our lives.

  Don't be too quick to judge others by this parable. It's not as easy as it seems. As well, there can be movement from one level to another. Ah ha. Pay close attention. It is brilliant in its simplicity.

- Like it or not, it is part of our nature to sometimes feel like we're a little bit better than the rest of the world, either because of some good deeds we've done or because we've been able to accumulate more of life's physical treasures than the average person. Should this be the case, and we orient ourselves to this belief and lifestyle, we need to be careful of what is sometimes called getting our "comeuppance".

  There is no better illustration than in The Parable of The Rich Man and Lazarus. What begins ostensibly as a very clear demonstration of man's inhumanity to man, makes a dramatic turn, with an ending that was not foreseeable, and a lesson you will never forget. It reads like a powerful novel. Luke 16: 19-31.

So, this is like an Amazon Book Store, where they say, if you like this, then try this one, too. Well, along with the wonderful, educational, and spiritually challenging parables we've just looked at, the Bible is full of many more that you won't want to miss, such as The Parables of The Talents, The Hidden Treasure, The Great

Banquet, The Barren Fig Tree (particularly good lesson), Wise and Foolish Builders, The Unjust Stewart, The Master and The Stewart, and many more. Enjoy and learn from all!!!

CHAPTER EIGHTEEN

God's Awesome Story

MIRACLES

The Divinity of Jesus Christ is illustrated frequently and brilliantly throughout the New Testament.

There is no better example of this than the many miracles He performed in front of sometimes thousands. Generally, the miracles were performed to either cure, feed, or improve onlookers in some often profound way.

These miracles were not done exclusively to heal and provide necessities for the citizens, but sometimes it was primarily to glorify His Father in a special way, as in the raising of Lazarus from the dead, and with dozens of onlookers, He spoke out loud to His Father, providing further evidence of His Divine being.

With the many naysayers who were the Pharisees, Levites, Scribes, and pagans, to help convince who He was and whom He said He was, The Son of God, the Messiah who had come to save the Israeli people and all mankind, He stated, in John 14:11, "Believe me when I say that I am in The Father, and The Father is in Me, or **at least believe on the evidence of the works (miracles) themselves**".

The following is merely a partial list of the miracles Christ performed as shown in The New Testament. Remember, even though these were performed by a Divine Being, Jesus Christ, everyone had reliable witnesses who authenticated the events, and have stood the test over centuries:

- Turned water into wine at a wedding in Cana
- Healed an official's deathly ill son in Capernaum
- Healed a paralytic at the pool of Bethesda
- Fed 5,000 people with five loaves of bread, and two fish
- Walked on water during a violent storm to join His disciples
- Healed a blind man in Bethsaida
- Raised Lazarus from the dead in Bethany
- Healed a woman from lifelong hemorrhaging
- Restored a severed ear from a high priest's servant
- Healed a man with a withered hand on the Sabbath
- Caused a fig tree to wither by merely speaking to it
- And last BUT NOT LEAST, was the miracle of His resurrection from the dead. He then appeared to hundreds of people, including His disciples, for forty more days on earth, before ascending into Heaven to join His Father.

Wow, Wow, and Amen to That!

APPENDIX ONE

CONSCIENCE OR CONSEQUENCES

Consider for a moment, what it would be like if there were no rules regulating all the traffic on our streets. No stop signs, no red lights, no yield signs, no lane markers, no speed limits, no pedestrian-protected crosswalks. It would, of course, be utter chaos! Nobody would be safe. Death and damage would prevail.

Now, think back if you can, 3,700 years ago, on Mt. Sinai, when God handed down a similar set of rules, called the Ten Commandments, but this time, as a guide to human behavior. Rules that were intended to set parameters on what is harmful, dangerous, but also, refreshing, and lifesaving. It would seem to make sense, that if we were to benefit, not only in this life but for all eternity thereafter, that we would take these guidelines, these rules of living, very seriously.

Well, over the centuries, just as happened 3,700 years ago, some people took them seriously, and some did not. We can only presuppose the inevitability of the consequences of ignoring these rules. Just as in the example of having no traffic regulations, chaos, injury, suffering, and even death would be the ultimate results. It appears that is the direction we are headed.

With our "politically correct" politicians demanding a more and more secular society, removing all possible images, remnants, verbiage, signs, or speech that relate to the Ten Commandments, we are returning to that age 3,700 years ago, when there were no rules, no discipline, no morals, no respect for each human being. Only power, greed, sexual promiscuity, debauchery, and survival of the fittest. Sound familiar?

How did being "politically correct" completely circumvent being "morally correct"? Who gave these promoters of secularism the right and the power to demote, trash, and dismantle all semblance of the moral code that has lasted for so many thousands of years? Well, I guess you and I are to blame.

Just curious: If someone entered your home, without permission, would you do everything in your power to reject them? If one of your children were threatened harm, how would you react? If someone decided that your automobile should be theirs, not yours, would you fight to keep what is rightfully yours? If so, why don't you fight to save the very guidelines, the only moral code established by God Himself, from being trashed? And if you have any spirituality as a cornerstone of your beliefs, by letting the Ten Commandments be denounced, set aside, and eliminated, you are not only contributing to a monstrous "spiritual traffic wreck", but you are endangering the very essence of an afterlife, which is pre-eminent in all Christian, and Jewish theology.

Think this is all "Chicken Little" crying the sky is falling? Just re-read the history of the Rise and Fall of the Roman Empire, and make your own determination if the decay and ignoring of any and all civil, human guidelines with a moral foundation could happen in the United States today with similar consequences.

Let's take a closer look at what is contributing to this horrific reversal in our acceptance and daily performance of our commitment to our faith(s).

#1. "I am the Lord thy God, you shall not have strange Gods before you." Think about Hollywood. Look at all the awards they give to themselves, and live and die by the results. They place themselves above the masses and profess to be elite in their attitudes towards our spirituality and daily lives. Look at the incredible wealth that Wall Street creates for themselves. The CEO of a company is being taken over by another rival company and is going to receive half a billion dollars as he goes out the door. Money rules. And, look at our politicians. Every day, it seems, we read yet another story of one or more of them putting themselves not only above the law, but putting them on a pedestal for all to honor and admire. How about the power and ubiquity of social media, particularly with our kids? There have been repeated stories of kids committing suicide because of what was said about them on a social site. What false Gods are all these folks following??

#2. "Love thy neighbor as thy self". You don't have to look in horror just at the jihadists beheading people, indiscriminately to see man's inhumanity to man at its worst. Just look at how we treat our own people. It is estimated that over 1.5 million people are currently homeless in the US. Ever walk by someone lying on the sidewalk, sleeping under a bridge or in a public park, and simply wondering what will become of them while doing nothing yourself? Rampant racism, by all races, is an ugly social cancer, with terrible results. How about the last time you had a disagreement with a family member, friend, or foe? Ever think about the same reconciliation and forgiveness you are afforded by Christ because of your faith being extended to those persons?

#3. "Thou shalt not kill". You don't have to have a long memory to recall and to realize this Commandment is violated every day, over and over. But, you don't have to look at these mass slayings to see the gut-wrenching effects of daily violence in cities like Chicago, where people are slaughtered as if they were simply a worthless piece of trash. In 2014, there were over 650,000 abortions, the killing of live human beings, in the United States. Why doesn't the child have a right to live, too? Unconscionable, but legal and largely acceptable in our secular society.

#4. "Thou shalt not steal". Theft is rampant in all parts of our society. Daily liquor store robberies, employees embezzling from their employers, Wall Street power brokers getting "inside information", and converting that into major personal gains at the loss of others, politicians misusing their donated funds, and casino employees skimming off the top. However, there are many other ways that stealing goes on that are equally as harmful: plagiarizing others' works, infringing on a patent, taking credit publicly or personally for something you did not originate, and promising someone something, then reneging. You can steal thoughts, money, dreams, dignity, opportunity, and decency from the rightful owners, and not even give it a second thought.

#5. "Thou shalt not covet thy neighbor's wife, nor goods". Angst over having less than your neighbor, in not only material goods, but possibly in good health, happiness, family, opportunity, faith, and overall lifestyle is completely debilitating to you, and only you. Value what gifts you have been given, and be happy for the gifts others have received that make their lives better, too.

#6. "Thou shalt not commit adultery". Began with the earliest of civilization, and continues unabated today. Where there are men and women, the temptation, and follow-through will continue. The sickness and spread of pornography, pedophilia, and other forms of perverse sexuality all contribute to this behavior. However, there are few things more destructive to the individual, our children, the family, the community, and the overall human population than adultery. It is popularized ad infinitum in the movies, novels, and theater. Look at how the proverbial dominoes have fallen when just one Hollywood starlet steps up and accuses a prominent Director of sexual improprieties. Others are quickly mentioned and then politicians, sports figures, and other high-profile individuals' reputations, and sometimes fortunes, come tumbling down. Unfortunately, only the fear of getting caught, the adverse financial consequences, and public ostracizing generally are the most likely concerns. Self-restraint and an acknowledgement and abiding by the absoluteness of this Command will obviate participation.

#7. "Do not bear false witness against thy neighbor". Consider for a moment the term, "perjury". Lying under oath. This is the quintessential use of bearing false witness, and when done so in a legal setting, is a crime in and of itself, with severe punishment. However, look at today's media. The accusations fly every day and the truth is either altered or outright fabricated, towards the intended detriment of a person or institution. Too often, there is no punishment, but spiritually, there has been a significant violation when this occurs, and will not go unpunished. As well, this happens every day with individuals, who, intentionally or unintentionally, distort information about another. It cannot be tolerated in a society with any kind of solid moral fiber.

The final three Commandments don't get as much attention as those listed above, but are nonetheless, no less important if you believe, in your heart and soul, that these all came from God Himself.

#8. "Do not use the Lord's name in vain". To use His name in vain is the ultimate disrespect, and show of arrogance towards the very Creator of not only this moral code, but of you, me, and the entire universe. Yet, it rolls off tongues in conversation every day, as if as a Commandment, it did not exist.

#9. "Honor thy father and mother". This should be such a natural, instinctive part of our families, and communities. The disrespect for parents, teachers, and other adults is manifested in behavior that causes hurt, harm, and ultimately failure. It is a societal breakdown that is curable with a proper moral attitude.

#10. "Keep holy the Sabbath day". How hard can this be? Ok, I hear you. This is the day I kick back, watch football, and play with the kids. In other words, refresh. But, what about refreshing your faith, and re-setting your moral compass?! One hour a week, out of 168 can't be too much of a burden if it can either keep you on some semblance of a decent course or change your life. It just may be setting a good example for your family, friends, and associates at work.

It is now critical to remember this. Newton's Law, which describes "for every action, there is an equal and opposite reaction" applies just as much to our morality, and code of conduct, as it did to Newton. If we allow our politicians, the Hollywood screenwriters, and the media, the morally corrupt elements of our culture, of our entire society, to tell us what we can and cannot believe in, and in fact practice that belief, both privately, and publicly, then shame on us. It is we, and generations to follow who will suffer the inevitable, and spiritually destructive consequences. Time to step up, and honor our God once again, just as He was meant to be.

Richard E. Tomlinson

APPENDIX TWO

JUST HOW POWERFUL IS THE WORD?

Picture this. You are sitting at your kitchen table and look down at a slice of bread on your plate. While it sits there, it of course is of no value to you. However, once you consume it, it becomes part of you. It nourishes and enriches your whole body.

The written and spoken word directs and even commands virtually everything we think and do each moment of our lives. It teaches us, encourages as well as discourages us, directs and informs us, challenges, excites, and even occasionally disappoints us. Without it, the world is one gigantic, hollow, empty space.

Now, envision this as well. You are standing in the street of a strange small town, somewhat lost and confused, and most anxious for someone to assist you and help unravel the complicated mess you find yourself in. Just then, a stranger comes by and offers a welcoming, and reassuring hand. You grasp his hand, and somehow, deep down you feel the comfort you are so desperately seeking.

This real-life drama did play out, several times over, in Jerusalem 2000 years ago. Can you possibly imagine yourself standing there, holding the hand of Jesus, the living Son of God

Himself?? What would you say? What would you ask Him? Would you take seriously what He was talking about? Would you follow His suggestions? Would you understand His wisdom? Would this encounter in any way affect or change your life?

The Gospel of John says that Jesus Himself was The Word. Yes, the very power of the Word began and continues to be, the Son Of God. The people of Jerusalem were introduced to Him in person and listened to His spoken word. However, prophets for many millennia had previously anticipated these rare events and had committed them in writing. Who believed them? And then their prognostications all came true. Were the people ready? No.

Fortunately, we have a powerful, meticulous, detailed, and convincing written proof that can grasp not only our hands, but our minds and very souls, and help lead us in that direction that will lead to eternal life. Yes, the Bible. There is No Substitute.

>   Blessings, Richard E. Tomlinson

APPENDIX THREE

THE UNIMAGINABLE REALLY HAPPENED

Our collective life experiences simply don't prepare us for what happened today. We were advised, and ostensibly prepared for this event, yet many of us, like our predecessors, either failed to understand or accept the realities and the inevitable consequences.

Brilliant philosophers and prophets wrote this day was coming for over 3,000 years, and now here it is. Now what? There remains hate, and havoc everywhere throughout the world. To what end? Greed, pride, power, indulgence, and sexual obsession prevail. To whose benefit? Much suffering continues, unabated. There must be an answer, and fortunately for every one of us, there is.

The human mind struggles to comprehend how one person, yes just one person could possibly help solve these life dilemmas and difficulties, but nonetheless, it happened. The problem we all have had, and many continue to have as well, is making sense of the message and life of this one person. The reason for the lack of understanding? We continue to try and solve life's problems through purely intellectual pursuits. What we are missing is that the answer must come from the heart. Yes, the heart.

Richard E. Tomlinson

The mind is a beautiful gift, but unless it is open to the intangible powers of the heart, it is just another piece of physical matter, that we use to propel ourselves into the morass we call life.

Therefore, it is only if we combine the mind and the heart, can we possibly begin to feel, and understand how this one person, Jesus Christ could love, and then suffer immeasurable pain for our bad behavior, and many sins. Wow! Think about your own life. Think about many of the biblical figures: Peter, Paul, Moses, and others…they were major sinners. They killed people, denied Christ's divinity, and imprisoned innocent people, yet they became the collective cornerstones of the Christian faith, which is based on forgiveness, and love.

Today, Christ was resurrected from death and literally reappeared to His chosen disciples shortly thereafter. Of this fact, there are many witnesses who have testified to this being factually correct.

The world, 3,000 years ago was just as corrupt as it is today. People are still treating other people in unconscionable ways. How then could a sovereign God, send His only Son to this earth, to love and save His people? It's because as our Creator, He loves us unconditionally, and wants us to join Him in an everlasting eternity. His extraordinary suffering shows us a love that is almost unimaginable. But it is real. Just open your heart, and let His love flow in. Peace, oh my what a beautiful peace.

Blessings to all, Richard

APPENDIX FOUR

LONELINESS IS AN EPIDEMIC STATES THE US SURGEON GENERAL. IS HE RIGHT?

On a recent visit to my Primary Care Physician's office, I was handed the usual clipboard, with several forms to fill out. A new one caught my eye: How is your emotional stability? It then proceeded to ask twenty questions such as: Are you lonely? Are you depressed? Do you feel ignored? Are you suicidal?

Ostensibly, these are all legitimate questions. But where are the answers, should any of these conditions be adversely impacting my life? There were only two: seek professional guidance, and/or submit your mind and body to some form of drug treatment. Ouch, seems like the only solutions are, in effect, creating another dependency.

However, I submit, there is a much more powerful, lasting, and satisfying solution. (Stay with me, now…this Really works!). The same Creator who brought you onto this earth loves you unconditionally and wants in every way to see you happy, and enjoying all the fruits of His labor. And He is ALWAYS AVAILABLE to comfort you, ease your pain, and help you solve the very problems that are causing your emotional distress.

Ten years ago, while sitting in a motel room I decided to pick up the Bible they had made available to each room. I opened it at random, and what I read changed my life. It was the first chapter of the Gospel of John. Since that day, I have begun every morning with a brief reading of Scripture, and it seems to irrevocably prepare me for whatever comes my way that day.

"Peace be with you, my peace I give to you". Yes, He means it. Take Him up on this promise. As well, it is quoted: "God so loved the world that He gave His only Son, so that all would have life eternal". Wow. How about that for a love that is so powerful, and redeeming, that you can not only count on it but let it relax all the tensions and turmoil in your life?

Now, this requires some participation on your part, too. And, it is incredibly easy and eternally rewarding. It begins with taking a deep breath, letting your shoulders relax, and having total confidence you are on the right track to a fulfilling, life-changing experience.

The next step is opening your heart to a love you never thought possible, and all the benefits that accrue from this new relationship. The final and most important component is you must have Faith that all this is real and that your life will forever change for the better.

However, this all takes patience, and as you pray, and find unqualified solace in His Word and promise, gradually the demands and stresses of life become much less controlling, as you now have a new source to direct and guide your thinking, actions, and outcomes. You now have an Advocate.

To be able to hand over all your trauma, and anxiety to a superior power, without drugs or other artificial stimulants, seems like the perfect solution. And it is. Try it. You will never regret your decision.

Richard E. Tomlinson

APPENDIX FIVE

BONO, AND U2'S LAMENT. THE FINAL CONNECTION

I don't know if you have been as fascinated, and intrigued as I have been over the years, of listening to the lyrics of U2's "But I still haven't found what I'm looking for". Powerfully written, with heartfelt lyrics, they share a life journey that most of us have traveled or may be still in the process of traveling.

For me, there are two elements of this song that are most impactful. First, the lyrics say: "I have climbed the highest mountains, run, crawled, scaled city walls, ONLY TO BE WITH YOU. But, yes, I'm still running".

This dramatic personal search then adds: "I believe in the Kingdom come, then all the colors will bleed into one. You broke the chains, CARRIED THE CROSS of my shame, you know I believe it".

However, after the agony of this personal pursuit to find a genuinely spiritual, life-supporting, and deeply satisfying meaning to life, the song ends with, "And I still haven't found what I'm looking for".

I have a sense, however, that he (Bono) really DID find it, he just couldn't quite make the final connection.

Of course, virtually all of us are, or have been in a continual search for that "final connection". During life's journey, the combination of joys, and sorrows shape and influence our perception and pursuit of a substantive answer to the question, "Is there really a God, and if so, how can I find Him?" During that search, we often share a similar lament to the lyrics mentioned above, as we go headfirst into driving, and climbing proverbial walls, in either a desperate pursuit of the "final connection", or we are taking a more contemplative approach by reading, praying, and meditating.

Recently, I came across a Biblical quote that may help answer that question. It is from the Book of Matthew, Chapter 19:13–15. Christ is speaking to the Apostles, who have errantly tried to keep the small children from interfering with their time with Him. Christ then says, "Let the children come to me, and do not prevent them, for the Kingdom of heaven belongs to such as these". Yes, that is the SAME KINGDOM mentioned in the U2 song.

What was Christ's message here? Children, of course, are innocent, trusting, dependent, and open to His guidance. So essentially, He is saying that throughout our life's pursuits of meaning and purpose, the total confidence in Christ in a childlike manner is how we can finally find that "connection".

If we are fortunate to live long enough, we will have innumerable opportunities for insights into that which we are all seeking. Some will understand this more quickly than others. Some people will, unfortunately, never get it, or worse, reject it out of hand. When you DO feel it and sense it, embrace it with all your heart. It just may be the "meaning" you are looking for.

Richard E. Tomlinson

APPENDIX SIX

HOMELESS

Pray for me, pray for me he said, as he spoke very quietly and leaned back his head.

His eyes marbled with a lifetime of hurt, his shoes, clothes, and face, stained with dirt.

Hands very leathery, cracked and bleeding. Grasping free food, somewhat nourishing and forgiving.

Hands that squeeze, extend friendship, that wave and hold. Caring not whether you are young or old.

"Beggars and bums", go to work they say. Would you hire me? Would they, try as I may?

I'm confused I realize, as to what life means, But surely it's not as today it seems.

With corporate edifices rising high above, amongst all the marble and concrete, is there still room for love.

For all the gifts we're given, are meant to share and passed on to benefit all, by those who care.

For in God's image was I along with you, created to follow His word, and to Him be true.

To you, to me, and to our fellow man, help me, help me be all that I can.

I beg you for neither sympathy nor sorrow, but hold tightly to each other, for today and tomorrow.

And pray my flight not be yours one day, at which time on my knees, for your wellbeing I'll pray.

Compassion is lasting, more so than greed, so can we join together in our common day of need.

I ask not for that which I've not earned, but only for life's blessings , as all we have yearned.

My children, too, suffer as I attempt to provide, some semblance of self respect, as life is no free ride.

But living in rooms, that from day to day change, Believe my best intentions, and ultimately limit their life's range.

I'm just like you, with hopes and pain, I commit everyday to at least sustain.

If Not Now, When?

My crippled dignity, my self-image and worth. That's been a part of me, ever since my birth.

Daylight rises, at least one more time, and dreams revert back to reality as the sun begins to shine.

For today is no different than yesterday or tomorrow. The endless cycle continues mixing optimism and sorrow.

Look here deep down in my soul, please understand that failure was never my goal.

But given the chance I hope to someday rebound, and under the foundation of my life, once again gain some solid ground

Therefore, I ask only one single thing from you, not forgiveness, nor sympathy, nor hand outs, too.

Please give me the very simplest respect that you can. For I too, am God's creature, I too, am a man.

Richard E. Tomlinson

APPENDIX SEVEN

KELLY: WHEN IS A HANDICAP A GIFT?

Several years ago, I was asked to share a brief opening message with my church, at the beginning of the Lenten Season. Struggling to immediately find a subject that might be inspiring to 1,400 people since I was simply one of the lay parishioners, I wrestled with the opportunity for several days.

A personal challenge of considerable concern I had for many years was the fact that one of my daughters, Kelly, who was by then an adult, was born with severe brain damage, and was not capable of dressing herself, let alone being able to read or understand any of the complex stories and messages of the Bible. To my way of thinking, and that of my faith, my lament was that she would never share in the intimate love of Christ with which I had become blessed. How could she? She was irreversibly handicapped. Or was she?

Knowing that I would be looking into the faces of these 1,400 people, was my message to be about what someone was NOT able to do, or what impact even a developmentally disabled person like

Kelly could have on all of us? Essentially, then, even with her handicaps, could she teach us anything?

As I sat reviewing the Ten Commandments, the answer suddenly came into focus. There is no human being alive that has not violated one or more of the Commandments, either on an occasional or frequent basis. Sometimes it is done unintentionally, sometimes it is done with full recognition of the violation, with malice, and without regard to the consequences. That is, with the possible exception of Kelly, and others who are similarly handicapped.

You see, to me, as you and I go about our daily lives making decisions as to whether what we do will benefit or harm others, regardless of the moral issues at hand, that is not the same with Kelly. As I had struggled with her "possible" lack of knowledge of Christ's life, suffering, love, and forgiveness, a new truth dawned on me.

She has never intentionally violated any, not one, of the Ten Commandments. Wow, that flipped the original concept upside down. It was then that I realized that MY DREAM OF KELLY BEING MORE LIKE US WAS MISGUIDED. RATHER, WE SHOULD STRIVE TO BE MORE LIKE KELLY.

Richard E. Tomlinson

www.ingramcontent.com/pod-product-compliance
Lightning Source LLC
LaVergne TN
LVHW010417220326
834503LV00025B/427